The Mode

Jo

The Modern Spirituality Series

Henri Nouwen

Metropolitan Anthony of Sourozh

John Main

Lionel Blue

John Main

A selection of his writing made by
Clare Hallward
with an Introduction by
Laurence Freeman
and arranged for daily reading

TEMPLEGATE PUBLISHERS

First published in 1987 by
Darton, Longman and Todd Ltd
89 Lillie Road, London SW6 1UD

ISBN 0-87243-166-5

First published in the United States in 1988 by

Templegate Publishers
302 E. Adams St./P.O. Box 5152
Springfield, Illinois 62705

The cover photograph of René Magritte's
"The Tempest" is reproduced
with the permission of the Wadsworth Atheneum,
Hartford, Connecticut. Bequest of Kay Sage Tanguy.

Cover Design: Scott Turner

John Main

Contents

Note

My husband and I first met Dom John Main in the autumn of 1980 in Montreal. He had about him an integrity and an inner authority which we learned came from the fact that he lived what he talked about. Later, as we came to know him as a friend, we grew to appreciate his warmth, his humour and that Irish flair for storytelling.

I started to collect extracts from his books and tapes as preparation for a retreat I was asked to lead. This was so interesting that I decided to pursue not only the core of what he was saying —as I understood it—but also to try to touch upon the full range and scope of his teaching.

I have thoroughly enjoyed the work of selecting and putting together these excerpts. On page 95 there is a full list of the books they were taken from for any reader who would like to dig deeper.

CLARE HALLWARD
Montreal
January 1987

INTRODUCTION

The recent history of the Church is the record of Christianity encountering or confronting modern consciousness. Not all would agree on the merits of modern consciousness or even on what it is, but anyone involved in the responsibilities of contemporary life and who has any sense of tradition feels that there is a quality of awareness around that is new in history. When it first confronted modernity, Christianity sensed an enemy. It threw itself against the advancing line of modern thinkers, writers, artists and activists and found itself frequently repulsed. Wounded, but ever pragmatic, it made concessions which some Christians saw as betrayals, others as brave signs of an unexpected renaissance of faith. Its encounter with modernity challenged Christianity, as one of the oldest and most taken-for-granted institutions of the West, to confront itself in a non-institutional way, with a non-authoritarian relationship to itself and the world. In other words, modernity has consistently brought the Church to deeper self-knowledge and to a humility that its history has not accustomed it to.

This has involved an institutional catastrophe in many parts of the Church – a collapse of conventional practice of the faith in Europe, for example, to fourteen per cent of the baptized. Naturally, when such a process is seen only in terms of institutional structures, people look to see 'where we have gone wrong' and 'what we can recover'. Having embarked upon its own self-

revolution in the Second Vatican Council the
Roman Catholic Church lost some of its revol-
utionary confidence and began to stiffen itself
again against the modernity which it had only just
begun to sense was not purely hostile to itself. But,
once gained, this insight – source of hope and
humour – can never be completely lost: that in
the supposed enemy of modernity the Christian
Church will find mirrored essential elements of its
own true self and so of its destiny.

Those who have seen the reflection of the future
in the meanings of today are the teachers of
modern Christianity. They are messengers of hope
for the great project of passing on the faith, generation to generation, in such a way that the faith
expands and develops in every act of transmission.
When these acts are remembered, history comes
to be; and in Christian history the most significant
individuals in any epoch have always been the
saints and teachers rather than the ecclesiastical
politicians and administrators. It is the teachers
we need to attend to most seriously today.

This book gives us an opportunity to do this.
Clare Hallward has sensitively and intelligently
selected passages and sentences from the teaching
of one of the most important of modern Christian
teachers. It is a book to be read more than once,
to be kept readily at hand, not as a way of
escaping the demands of modern living but of
discovering how to meet this challenge with Christian hope. If it is read as it is meant to be read it
will lead you to read the books from which it
derives its content, the books in which John Main
passed on his teaching about the renewal of

modern Christian life through the tradition of Christian meditation. And if you read these books – where you will encounter the authority of a true teacher – and learn what they are saying through your own experience, they will lead you to a deeper life of prayer and a richer life in Christ.

The format of this book is particularly appropriate, considering the kind of teacher John Main was. Monastic teachers – and John Main also serves as a model of the modern Christian monk – have an especially strong sense of the personal nature of the act of transmission of faith. For them the locus of learning is not the classroom but the family of the monastery which St Benedict described as a 'school of the Lord's service'. Monks are trained in a wisdom tradition rather than a scholastic one and this emphasizes the personal bond between teacher and pupil rather than the objectivity of the relationship between a lecturer and his class. Naturally this distinction highlights a perennial source of tension and paradox in the monastery as well as in the Church, one that incidentally reinforces the claim of monasteries to be microcosms of the universal Church. Christianity, like every human organization, struggles with the polarities of the personal and the communal, the charismatic and the institutional, the prophetic and the administrative.

Monasticism has not always been at ease with this tension and John Main's biography* describes a modern version of this problem. Somewhere between the highly individualized monasticism of

*Neil McKenty, *In the Stillness Dancing: The Journey of John Main* (Crossroad 1987).

the Egyptian Fathers, the collective spontaneity of the Celtic monks and the corporate stability of Benedict's Rule, the monastic archetype hovers. A monastic teacher such as John Main intuitively resists the institutionalization of monastic life and in his resistance discovers a way of affirming the perennial greenness of the shoots of Christian faith. John Main saw how great is the need today for men and women of deep prayer who will be true teachers at every level of the Church's life.

Hierarchies are innately suspicious of gurus, always and everywhere. The Christian teacher, however, has a special dimension to his or her charism that represents more than a cultural difference from the Eastern teaching traditions. In the East the transmission of the teaching through a lineage of teachers has little to correspond to the Christ-Teacher who enfolds and transcends the line of his disciples. Every Christian teacher is a disciple of Christ, the *sadguru*, and his and her growth is a deepening awareness of the union that exists between the master and the disciple, allowing thoughts and words and even experience to be transferred between the subjects of a unified consciousness. 'We, however, possess the mind of Christ.'

Tradition is not what *has been* done but what *is being* lived in continuity with the past and in a hopeful thrust towards the future. The word itself, *traditio*, means a 'passing on', a 'transmission'. Christian faith is effectively lost, though the structures of Christianity may remain powerful for a while, when tradition becomes archaic rather than a contemporary reappropriation and projection forward. What is being regained and passed on is not something that can replace the necessity of our personally experiencing it. The life of a tradition is precisely this multiple personal experience forming and awakening the ecclesial reality. Experience and tradition are inseparably integrated in John Main's teaching and his insistence on the need for 'personal verification of the truths of our faith'.

These sentences of his teaching suggest the brevity, directness and simplicity of a monastic teacher. The richness of their truthfulness is movingly set in their poverty of form. As a form of teaching they are part of a tradition that has its roots in prehistory and in the origins of the Christian oral transmission. The apophthegms or sayings of the Desert Fathers distilled the wisdom that springs from the confluence of tradition and personal experience. Their disciples would come and ask, 'Abba, give us a word' and the word would be a short, easily memorized saying which they would take away, ruminate over, work on, until its meaning had sunk from the head into the heart from where it would flow into their whole being.

Such a way of learning is practically incomprehensible to us in our cerebral exile. Not only do we associate knowledge with power, we think that knowledge increases in proportion to data. Scholarship, for us, leads to truth rather than being a service or liturgy of truth. But, however we regard education and the search for wisdom, human beings learn through a basic method of repetition (imitation), and exploration (practice). Modern education tends to ask for nothing more than an adequate regurgitation of facts and instilled opinions. Christian teaching, by contrast, does not achieve its goal until the disciple, without ceasing to be a learner, becomes one who has so deeply and personally *understood* what he has learned that he can now teach with the authority of brevity and, ultimately, of silence.

Christian tradition originated in the handing-down of the sayings of Jesus. Jesus taught within a religious culture that gave as much importance to economy of expression (such as the distillation of theology into the daily ritual prayers or the phrases of the Our Father and the Beatitudes) as it did to elaborate and painstaking exegesis of Scripture. The former orients us to prayer, the latter towards thought. It is important to see these two different activities as being united by a common spectrum of consciousness. We are capable of thought and of prayer and of thinking about prayer. But, significantly, we do not talk about praying about thought. To pray is to be moving in a particular and humanly inevitable direction along the spectrum of our being. Prayer becomes increasingly unself-reflective and silent, purer in its freedom from images and concepts. Prayer is, as John Main repeatedly said, a journey. This perception about 'pure prayer' underlies one of the most memorable of the Fathers' sayings, one of St Anthony's:

> The monk who knows that he is praying is not truly praying. The monk who does not know that he is praying is truly praying.

Only when we modern Christians understand –

16

and only experience will teach us – what St Anthony meant by 'knowing' and 'praying' and how his meaning differs by its breadth from ours, will we recover what has been lost from the tradition that still unites us across the intervening sixteen hundred years.

It is in this context of spiritual knowledge that the significance of John Main's *remembering* of the Christian tradition of the mantra must be understood. His own experience first touched the tradition in its universal, pre-Christian manifestation after he had learned from a Hindu monk how to meditate. What awakened him to his relationship to his teacher was not a book or a lecture but a short saying from the Upanishads:

He contains all things, all works and desires and all perfumes and tastes. And he enfolds the whole universe and, in silence, is loving to all. This is the Spirit that is in my heart. This is Brahman.

The Benedictine monastic tradition later reconnected John Main's experience to the Christian teaching on meditation. With his experience of the missing element, he was able to see the way things held together in connectedness on the spectrum. He saw that the reading of Scripture, vocal liturgical prayer, theology, community living and the active expression of love in Christian vocation are not in contradiction to the 'pure prayer' of the tradition. All make up a whole in which each part is vitally necessary to the others.

Yet the harmony of the different elements of Christian life is not static. It promotes growth

17

towards a goal in which love integrates all the parts. In the Christian vision the love experienced in the times of meditation and the love we experience, giving and receiving as always with love, in the times of interaction is the one and the same love. At each stage of growth and at each successive level of integration this love appears to us as Christ more fully realized in his glorified humanity.

The mantra – or *formula*, as Cassian called it – is like a template, meant to order and harmonize consciousness. It is not an unconnected, free-floating technique. The way many modern people approach it as a discipline of prayer probably mirrors how it developed prehistorically into the precise and radically simple teaching John Main recognized, remembered and further developed. The mantra is a short word or phrase repeated continuously throughout the time of meditation. Cassian recommended a verse of the Psalms, *The Cloud of Unknowing*, the name of God. John Main suggested an ancient Aramaic Christian prayer quoted by St Paul: *maranatha*. There is nothing magic or esoteric about choosing or, more traditionally, being given, your mantra. The saying of the mantra is an act of faith, faith active in the love of leaving ourselves behind to enter more fully into the experience, that is to say, the Spirit of Christ. But to make this faith absolute, this loss of self total, we are taught with the authority – both of wisdom and of commonsense – the importance of taking one mantra, not changing it from time to time or during the meditation, and of reciting it *continuously* in a spirit of humble and unself-analytical simplicity.

As soon as we begin to practise this discipline we encounter the radical demand of poverty of spirit. A rationalizing spirit of compromise soon appears and there is a strong temptation to adjust the teaching to meet our own present capacity for silence and stillness even though this involves a depreciation of our potential capacity. So it can seem better, then, to change one's mantra to suit one's moods, to answer a felt need for religious meaning, to say the mantra discontinuously as we feel the need. Immediately, but superficially, prayer becomes easier. The process of moving beyond egoism, of leaving self behind, is comfortably suspended or postponed. We begin to love our life again rather than lose it. The journey is not stopped completely – life goes on – but it grinds into a painfully slow gear.

The problem here is that this approach to prayer – an approach that enshrines the observing and possessive ego instead of casting it from its throne – is regressive at the level at which we pray at depth 'in spirit and in truth'. The deeper and more spiritual our prayer becomes, the more we experience interiority and the more necessary it becomes to unhook consciousness from the ego and its complex little dramas. Otherwise, we will be deepening our introverted self-absorption while thinking perhaps that we are spiritually maturing. People sometimes ask if there is any danger involved in meditation. The only danger is that we remove our hand from the plough once we have begun, that we look back, that we stop saying the mantra.

At other levels of consciousness, at other times of our religious life, other approaches are obviously appropriate. In reading Scripture we savour and linger over the images and concepts. We read them, pause, go back and read again. Quite likely each *lectio* period will lead us to select one particular phrase or verse. From such experience, described by the earliest monastic writers, we can see how naturally a mantra appears. Through the process of progressive simplification and concentration which controls spiritual growth we are led to the 'single verse' of Cassian and on into the grand poverty of setting one's mind on the Kingdom before everything else. The beauty of a butterfly, never resting in its search for nectar, is shortlived. The beauty of humanity increases as we become still in the knowledge of God. From the many verses, sayings and apophthegms that express the teaching we select one to lead us into the stillness where we encounter the teacher.

Mankind is being impelled by its self-generated crisis today to meet itself, to discover the wholeness of its many families. Dialogue can initiate this meeting but only a common experience can complete it. It is a stage of our evolution and like all such transitions it has the ambiguity of the Chinese character for crisis: danger and opportunity. Religious, political and cultural differences can divide or enrich us depending on the quality of our underlying experience of unity. Human beings recognize this unity in some of the basic experiences of human life: birth, love and beauty, death. But this recognition is too subjective to save us. We need to recognize and embrace it in the most basic of all human experiences which is also the most developed – the experience of prayer, where human subjectivity is transcended in the personal God of love.

Of all the world's religious families, Christianity has most directly and courageously encountered modernity. It is shaking her institutions to their foundations but also proving the vitality and contemporaneity of her tradition. No one can be a Christian today without sensing the power of resurrection at work in the mortal structures of the Church.

Of the many words God has spoken through many religions and teachers only one became incarnate. He does not cancel out the other revelations but embodies and focuses them all. So the mantra, in the teaching of John Cassian and John Main, excludes nothing but includes every movement of the heart and mind and turns the whole person towards God. So also Christ turns humanity directly towards God.

In prayer within the community of faith, we discover Christ to be the Word of Truth. We find that the Word is not an idea but a truth-experience, an event of meeting that jumps the interpersonal gap, the alienation of the human condition. We find that the Truth is not an object or merely an answer but an enlightenment, an unveiling and a liberation from the cell of ignorance and illusion. To meet the Word of Truth is, then, to share in a life larger than our own circumscribed reality: to share in the very being of God.

The words of John Main flow from his experience of this meeting, from his own enlightenment and vitalization. They point us towards the same encounter in our own experience. It is our deepest personal and collective responsibility today to enter this experience.

LAURENCE FREEMAN OSB
Montreal
January 1987

THE GREAT COSMIC
RIVER OF LOVE

There is really only one prayer

The central message of the New Testament is that there is really only one prayer and that is the prayer of Christ.

It is a prayer that continues in our hearts day and night. It is the stream of love that flows constantly between Jesus and his Father. It is the Holy Spirit.

It is the most important task of any fully human life to become as open as possible to this stream of love. We have to allow this prayer to become our prayer, to enter into the experience of being swept beyond ourselves into this wonderful prayer of Jesus – this great cosmic river of love.

In order for us to do this we must learn a most demanding discipline that is a way of silence and stillness.

It is as though we have to create a space within ourselves that will allow the consciousness of the prayer of Jesus to envelop us in this powerful mystery.

The eye that cannot see itself

We are used to thinking of prayer in terms of 'my prayer' or 'my praise' of God, and it requires a complete rethinking of our attitude to prayer to see it as a way through Jesus, with Jesus, and in Jesus.

The first requirement is that we understand that we must pass beyond egoism, so that 'my' prayer is no longer even a possibility.

We are summoned to see with the eyes of Christ and to love with the heart of Christ; to respond to this summons we must pass beyond egoism.

In practical terms this means learning to be so still and silent that we cease thinking about ourselves, and this is of critical importance. We must be open to the Father through Jesus, and in prayer we must become like the eye that can see but that cannot see itself.

The way we set out on this pilgrimage of 'other-centredness' is to recite a short phrase, a word that is today commonly called a mantra.

The mantra is simply a means of turning our attention beyond ourselves, a way of unhooking us from our own thoughts and concerns.

Absorbed in the mystery of God

Reciting the mantra brings us to stillness and to peace. We recite it for as long as we need to before we are caught up into the prayer of Jesus. The general rule is that we must first learn to say it for the entire period of our meditation each morning and each evening, and then to allow it to do its work of calming over a period of years.

A day will come when the mantra ceases to sound and we become lost in the eternal silence of God. The rule when this happens is not to possess this silence or to use it for one's own satisfaction.

As soon as we consciously realize that we are in this profound silence and then begin to reflect about it we must gently and quietly return to our mantra.

Gradually the silences become longer and we are simply absorbed in the mystery of God. The important thing is to have the courage and generosity to return to the mantra as soon as we become self-conscious of the silence.

Each of us is summoned to the heights of Christian prayer, to the fullness of life. What we need, however, is the humility to tread the way very faithfully over a period of years so that the prayer of Christ may indeed be the grounding experience of life.

Freedom and frankness

As our society becomes increasingly less religious its need for the authentically spiritual intensifies.

Religion is the sacred expression of the spiritual but if the spiritual experience is lacking then the religious form becomes hollow and superficial and self-important. *Religion does yield high dividends, but only to the man whose resources are within him* [1 Tm 6:6].

How often does the violence with which men assert or defend their beliefs betray an attempt to convince themselves that they do really believe or that their beliefs are authentic? The spectre of our actual unbelief can be so frightening that we can be plunged into extreme, self-contradictory ways of imposing our beliefs on others rather than simply, peacefully, living them ourselves.

When religion begins to bully or to insinuate, it has become unspiritual because the first gift of the Spirit, creatively moving in man's nature, is freedom and frankness.

Presence

The principal criticism one might have of contemporary Christians is that we are and have been so slow to understand the full, present magnificence of the invitation to be wholly open to Christ.

Writing of this invitation to life St Paul says, 'It is God himself who has called you to share in the life of his Son Jesus Christ our Lord; and God keeps faith' [1 Co 1:9].

Our mission as modern Christians is to resensitize our contemporaries to the presence of a spirit within themselves.

It is not the tradition handed on to us from the past that gives meaning to the Presence. Instead, it is the Presence that fills the tradition with meaning.

The Church witnesses in every generation not to a system of dry doctrines but to the Presence of the living Christ in its midst and its principal message is that this living Presence is a wholly contemporary reality.

Inward renewal

The depth and nature of a radical renewal of spirit is not within our active power to bring about. What we have to do is to prepare ourselves for the power that will effect it.

Our preparation is our openness, our vulnerability to the power of God dwelling in us. This is prayer.

This means transferring our conscious hopes for a renewal of the Church's relevance and effectiveness in the world from politics to prayer, from mind to heart, from committees to communities, from preaching to silence.

Religious renewal is a renewal in prayer.

We are the Church

Modern man tends to see himself either as an anonymous part of the pattern unfolded to him daily in the newspapers and on the television or, more insidiously, as the impartial observer, the universal journalist or commentator.

The immediate task for the contemporary Christian is to see and experience ourselves as the Church. If the Church is failing to respond to the deep religious needs of our contemporaries it is because we, its people and ministers, fail in our personal response to Christ.

Our effectiveness in trying to turn back the tide of fear and hatred in the world depends upon our own insertion into the mystery of Christ.

The teaching Church

The challenge to the Church is the same one facing all men and women – to understand that the absolute is the only realism. Not only is it realistic, but it is the only way to come into contact with reality.

The Church cannot effectively proclaim a past experience. It can only proclaim what it is actually experiencing. It can only proclaim what *it is*.

If the gap between what we believe and what we experience makes us inauthentic, our message can convince no one until it has so convinced us that we are transformed by it.

A life that is not based on prayer, a Church that is not based on prayer, a world that is not based on prayer, cannot be a world, a Church or a life that is fully alive.

God's plan

One of the challenges we all face is to be continually sensitive to the unfolding of God's plan in our lives: to give free and open assent to the destiny his love is shaping for us.

It is so easy to lose that sensitivity. So much of our life is dominated by the mechanical, by the response that is expected or demanded of us, by attempts to predict or anticipate growth, that we are always in danger of losing contact with life as a mystery – and so with life itself.

Any fixed pattern we try to impose on our life falsifies the truth of the mystery that is eternally present and so unpredictable.

Our day-to-day life is of vital importance as the mystery of transformation is worked out in us and through us by the power of Christ. No detail is insignificant because the reassimilation of all creation in Christ is to be complete.

The plan being worked out in the life of each of us is the same as that being realized in all creation, the bringing into unity with Christ of all that is. The first sphere of this great movement into unity is the achievement of wholeness within ourselves.

One who begins alone will be joined by others

Once we begin the journey we receive so many strengths. The greatest strength is that the journey attracts fellow-travellers. One who begins alone will be joined by others. In that mystery of communion the Church is reborn and rekindled in many quiet corners of the earth.

However small the corner, it is born in its fullness because Christ is born there, humble, vulnerable, fully human. In those very qualities he brings us the fullness of the Father's love.

This is why the authentic Christian community, like Jesus himself, has always had an influence out of all proportion to its size and material power.

A *new creation*

The great conviction of the New Testament is that by giving us his Spirit Jesus has dramatically transformed the fabric of human consciousness. Our redemption by Jesus Christ has opened up for us levels of consciousness that can be described by St Paul only in terms of a totally new creation.

God became man so that man might become God, as the early Fathers of the Church expressed it. It is our destiny to be divinized by becoming one with the Spirit of God. Divinization is utterly beyond our imagination and our own powers of understanding to comprehend. But it is not beyond our capacity to experience it in love.

Staggering as this revelation is and feeble though our capacity may be to receive it, it is worked out through the ordinariness of our humanity and the ordinariness of our human life.

The big problem in Christianity is to *believe* it.

The central reality of our faith

In Chapter 5 of his Letter to the Romans Paul writes about what God has accomplished in the person of his Son, Jesus:

> Therefore, now that we have been justified through faith, let us continue at peace with God through our Lord Jesus Christ, through whom we have been allowed to enter the sphere of God's grace, where we now stand. Let us exult in the hope of the divine splendour that is to be ours ... because God's love has flooded our inmost heart through the Holy Spirit he has given us [Rm 5:1–5].

Just think about this language for a moment and consider the quite staggering claim it is making.

St Paul was no mere theorist. He was a passionate announcer of a real event that he was trying to make all men realize. His great conviction is that the Spirit of Jesus has been sent. This is the central conviction of our Christian faith; indeed our faith is a living faith precisely because the living Spirit of God dwells within us, giving new life to our mortal bodies.

WE ARE NOT LOOKING FOR
HIM: IT IS HE WHO HAS
FOUND US

We do not know how to pray

Many Christians have lost touch with their own tradition of prayer. We no longer benefit as we should from the wisdom and experienced counsel of the great masters of prayer. These masters have agreed that in prayer it is not we ourselves who take the initiative. We are not talking to God. We are listening to his word within us. We are not looking for him; it is he who has found us.

Walter Hilton expressed it very simply in the fourteenth century. He wrote, 'You yourself do nothing. You simply allow him to work in your soul' [*The Scale of Perfection*, Book 2, ch. 24]. The advice of St Teresa was in tune with this. She reminds us that all we can do in prayer is to dispose ourselves; the rest is in the power of the Spirit who leads us.

These teachers of prayer have the same experience which led St Paul to write that 'we do not even know how to pray, but the Spirit prays within us' [Rm 8:26]. He was not writing to specialists in prayer, but to husbands, wives, butchers and bakers.

Marriage and the spirit of obedience

Marriage and prayer are intimately related in Paul's vision of the Christian life.

In both prayer and marriage the call is to full selfhood by loss of self in the other. The giving of self must become total. Both prayer and marriage are creative of life because of the generosity and faith that enable us to lay down our lives in love.

I suppose it wouldn't be an exaggeration to say that one of the principal causes of the breakdown of so many marriages is a lack of the spirit of obedience.

No word in the religious vocabulary is so much misunderstood by our contemporaries as 'obedience'. Obedience is nothing else than the capacity to listen to the other. We stray from God when we lose this attentiveness and no amount of talking or thinking about God can truly substitute for this openness to him. The Latin root of 'obedience' is *ob-audire*, to hear, to listen. We are to be listeners.

Obedience here is in essence sensitivity, deep sensitivity to the other, to the others. The readiness to think, in the first place, of the other and not of oneself.

As you know, it is impossible for us to love one another unless we serve one another.

Mary – a figure of universal relevance

To our own era, intent upon a rediscovery of an inner life that has been largely dissipated in materialistic systems of thought and of society, an age seeking for an affirmation of the reality of the spiritual dimension in man, Mary is above all the symbol of a rich, healthy and creative interiority.

The essential Christian insight which Mary exemplifies in Luke's Gospel is poverty of spirit. This is purity of heart because it is unsullied by the intrusion of the egotistic will seeking for experience, desiring holiness, objectifying the Spirit or creating God in its own image. Mary reveals the basic simplicity of the Christian response in a poverty of spirit that consists in turning wholly to God, wholly away from self.

Detachment is only the counterpart to concentration. In Mary's gospel response, as in the dynamic of prayer, the condition of detachment is really a concentration upon the Reality that contains and perfects all things.

On every occasion where Jesus addresses her, Mary is confronted with the hard truth of prayer: 'The way of possession is the way of dispossession.' No mother has ever possessed her son less possessively than Mary and for that reason no other has been able to be as open to his experience.

The other-centredness of Mary

The confusion we tend to make in the West is between Mary's motherhood and her interiority. We have emphasized the attractive, consoling mother out of proportion to the God-centred spirit of prayer, her 'other-centredness'.

Because one side of Mary's many-faceted meaning has tended to predominate under the influence of Augustinian morality, her importance in the realm of sexual symbolism has been exaggerated. Because she became enmeshed in unclear minds with a particular society's understanding, or misunderstanding, of human sexuality, much more was written in *defence* of her virginity than in *proclamation* of her importance as a model for prayer.

Mary is one of the greatest expressions in any culture of the wholly fulfilled woman, complete in her motherhood, her womanhood, and complete too in her spiritual maturity. And because both are complete there is no real demarcation between them.

In Mary, as in Jesus, we see the expression of the essential correspondence between body and spirit which itself finds expression in the New Testament account of the ascension and, later, in the assumption.

Mary's purpose and meaning is to lead us to Jesus.

The Trinity

In our lives we attempt to live out and explore to its depths our invitation to enter into community with *the* community of love – the most holy Trinity.

The mutual presence and self-communication that is the love-force of the Trinity transcends difference but does not obliterate distinction. That is why our fear of union, of the loss of self, is so unfounded.

The wonder of union is that it does *not* obliterate, but is creative.

To be involved is to evolve.

Teilhard de Chardin puts it beautifully and simply when he says, 'Union differentiates'. In union the rich variety of the human mystery is apprehended as a reflection of the unbounded creativity of God.

The pearl of great price

The great grace that all of us have been given is to believe in Jesus Christ, to believe in his presence in our hearts and to believe that he invites each of us to enter into that presence. That is an extra-ordinary gift to have been given.

We have to learn, because it is a gift of such staggering proportions, to respond to it gradually, gently. When we begin we cannot fully understand the sheer magnificence and wonder of it. Each time we return to meditate we enter into that reality a little more deeply, a little more faithfully.

When we begin we probably find our way to medi-tation as one among many options that we have been looking at and it takes us time to find that this is *the pearl of great price*.

I do not wish to imply that meditation is the only way, but rather that it is the only way I have found. In my experience it is the way of pure simplicity that enables us to become fully, integrally aware of the Spirit Jesus has sent into our heart. This is the recorded experience of the mainstream of the Christian tradition from apos-tolic times down to our own day.

Death – a part of life

If we would become wise we must learn that we have here no abiding city [Heb 13:14].

To have life in focus we must have death in our field of vision. Within this vision we see life as preparation for death and death as preparation for life.

If we are to meet our own death with hope it must be a hope built not on theory or on belief alone but on experience. We must know from experience that *death is an event in life*, an essential part of any life which is lived as a perpetually expanding and self-transcending mystery.

Only the experience of the continuous death of the ego can lead us into this hope, into an ever-deepening contact with the power of life itself.

Only our own death to self-centredness can really persuade us of death as the connecting link in the chain of perpetual expansion, and as the way to fullness of life.

We must prepare for death

The only ultimate tragedy is a life that has not opened to eternal life.

In the Christian vision, death is not the all-important moment in our life. The supreme all-important moment in any life is the moment of full openness to Jesus. We have to take practical steps to put ourselves into readiness.

Anyone who meditates in faith knows that the journey within takes us out of ourselves. Saying the mantra is learning to die and to accept the eternal gift of our being in one and the same act.

Our being passes through various stages of life, through many deaths, but we can never slip out of *being*. God never withdraws the immortal gift of life he has given to us. This is the essential preparation we need *in experience* to face our own death without fear, without false consolation, with open minds and open hearts.

All death is death to limitation. If we can die to self we rise to an infinite liberty of love. This way of dying to the ego, the first death, is what we call prayer.

The Spirit in silence is loving to all

Every great spiritual tradition has known that the human spirit begins to be aware of its own Source only in profound stillness.

In the Hindu tradition the Upanishads speak of the spirit of the One who created the universe as dwelling in our heart. The same spirit is described as the One who in silence is loving to all.

In our own Christian tradition Jesus tells us that the Spirit who dwells in our heart is the Spirit of love.

The meeting of East and West in the Spirit is one of the great features of our time, but it can only be fruitful if it is realized on the level of deep prayer. This, surely, is also true of the union of the different Christian denominations.

The glorious liberty of the children of God

What our encounter with India and the East is teaching us is something we should never have forgotten – that the essential Christian experience is beyond the capacity of any cultural or intellectual form to express or contain. This is what St Paul called the 'glorious liberty of the children of God': no restriction.

This experience has to be restored to the heart of the Church if she is to face creatively the challenges before her: the challenge of the renewal of her contemplative religious life, the challenge of restoring unity in the Spirit with all Christian communions, the challenge of embracing non-Christian religions with the universal love of Christ which is already present in the hearts of all people and which she has a special duty to release and identify. To meet these challenges each one of us must be personally rooted in Jesus' personal experience of God and which he shares with us all through his Spirit.

We do not earn this experience or create it from our own resources; it is for us to prepare for the grace of its giving.

John Cassian (1)

We would not still be reading the Gospels or St Paul today, were it not true that the human experience of the Spirit is essentially the same at all times and in all traditions. This is so because it is, in essence, the same encounter with the redemptive love of God in Jesus Christ, who is the same yesterday, today and for ever.

Throughout Christian history, men and women of prayer have fulfilled a special mission in bringing their contemporaries, and even succeeding generations, to the same enlightenment, the same rebirth in Spirit that Jesus preached.

One of these teachers was John Cassian, in the fourth century, who has a claim to be one of the most influential teachers of the spiritual life in the West. His special importance as the teacher and inspirer of St Benedict and so of the whole of Western monasticism, derives from the part he played in bringing the spiritual tradition of the East into the living experience of the West.

John Cassian (2)

The real work of meditation is to attain harmony of body, mind and spirit. This is the aim given us by the psalmist: 'Be still and know that I am God.' To achieve this we use a very simple device. It is one that St Benedict drew to the attention of his monks as long ago as the sixth century by directing them to read the *Conferences* of John Cassian [The Rule of St Benedict, 42:6; 13; 73:14].

Cassian recommended anyone who wanted to learn to pray continually to take a single short verse and to repeat this verse over and over again. In his Tenth *Conference* [10:10] he urges this method of simple and constant repetition as the best way of casting out all distractions and monkey chatter from our mind, in order for it to rest in God.

'No one', Cassian said, 'is kept away from purity of heart by not being able to read nor is rustic simplicity any obstacle to it for it lies close at hand for all if only they will by constant repetition of this phrase keep the mind and heart attentive to God' [*Conference*, 10:14].

When I read Cassian on this, I am immediately reminded that the whole of his teaching on prayer is based on the Gospels. Jesus approved of the prayer of the sinner who stood at the back of the temple and prayed in the single phrase: 'Lord, be merciful to me a sinner, Lord be merciful to me a sinner.' He went home 'justified', Jesus tells us, whereas the Pharisee who stood at the front of the temple in loud eloquent prayer did not [Lk 18:9–14].

**NOT IN MANY WORDS
BUT IN A LITTLE WORD**

'The Cloud of Unknowing'

A thousand years after Cassian the English author of *The Cloud of Unknowing* recommends the repetition of a little word:

> We must pray in the height, depth, length, and breadth of our spirit, not in many words but in a little word [*The Cloud of Unknowing*, ch. 39].

He writes: 'I tell you the truth when I say that this work (of meditation) demands great serenity, an integrated and pure disposition in soul and body . . . God forbid that I should separate what God has coupled: the body and the spirit' [ibid., ch. 41, 48].

'Use this little word, and pray not in many words but in a little word of one syllable. Fix this word fast to your heart so that it is always there come what may. With this word you will suppress all thoughts' [ibid., ch. 7, 39].

In meditation we turn the searchlight of consciousness off ourselves, off a self-centred analysis of our own unworthiness. 'If memories of past actions keep coming between you and God,' says the author of *The Cloud of Unknowing*, 'you are resolutely to step over them because of your deep love for God' [ibid., ch. 6].

Christian meditation

Meditative prayer is not an intellectual exercise in which we reflect about theological propositions. In meditation we are not *thinking* about God at all, nor are we thinking of his Son, Jesus, nor of the Holy Spirit. In meditation we seek to do something immeasurably greater; we seek to *be with* God, to *be with* Jesus, to *be with* his Holy Spirit, not merely to think about them.

It is one thing to know that Jesus is the revelation of the Father; or that he is our way to the Father. But it is quite another thing to experience the presence of Jesus within us, to experience the power of his Spirit within us for it is *in that experience* that we are brought into the presence of his Father and our Father.

Holiness is not fundamentally a moral quality. It is rather the unique experience of Presence.

We cannot apprehend God by thinking about him

When we begin to meditate we take our place in a great tradition, a tradition of hundreds, indeed thousands of years. When we begin we have to be humble enough to accept the tradition on faith.

The mantra has been part of the Christian tradition of prayer from the beginning and the understanding that prayer is beyond the operations of the mind is to be found in every authoritative statement of that tradition.

We are all basically aware that we cannot apprehend God by thinking about him. The great danger in prayer is to cut God down to our own size in order to talk to him, making a convenient shoulder for us to cry on and a convenient idol, enabling us to avoid the abyss of his otherness.

What we should understand is both his utter transcendence and his utter closeness to us in his indwelling Spirit. It is to this understanding of prayer that we are led not by theory but practice. This is prayer without images ... that restricts itself to the repetition of a single verse, the 'prayer of poverty'.

A *new* confidence

Saying the mantra is as easy as falling off a wall! All you do is to begin to say it in your mind, then sound it, and next listen to the sound of it.

The only quality you require then is the simplicity to keep saying it. 'Unless you become as little children.'

What word does a child keep repeating? 'Abba, Father'. Each repetition is a new confidence established, not because the child *thinks* about it, but because the child *experiences* the relationship as *real*.

That is what the mantra is about – no thoughts, no imagination; only *Presence*.

A tree filled with monkeys

The Indian mystic Sri Ramakrishna, who lived in Bengal in the nineteenth century, used to describe the mind as a mighty tree filled with monkeys, all swinging from branch to branch and all in an incessant riot of chatter and movement.

Prayer is not a matter of adding to this confusion by trying to shout it down and covering it with another lot of chatter. The task of meditation is to bring all this mobile and distracted mind to stillness, silence and concentration, to bring it, that is, into its proper service. This is the aim given us by the psalmist: 'Be still and know that I am God' [Ps 46:10].

One of the first great lessons in humility is that we come to wisdom and stillness and pass beyond distraction, only through the gift of God. His prayer is his gift to us and all we have to do is to dispose ourselves by becoming silent. Silence is the essential human response to the mystery of God, to the infinity of God.

It is this understanding that has led so many today to the threshold of real prayer. The way of prayer is a way of ever-deeper, ever more generous silence.

'Maranatha'

The mantra that I recommend is 'Maranatha'. I recommend it because it is in Aramaic, the language Jesus himself spoke, and because it is probably the most ancient prayer in the Church: St Paul ends Corinthians with it, John ends Revelation with it, it can be found in the *Didache* and so forth.

Throughout *The Cloud of Unknowing* the author urges us to choose a word that is full of meaning; but that once we have chosen it, we turn from the meaning and associations and listen to it as a sound. 'Maranatha' is a perfect mantra from that point of view.

Say the word gently but deliberately in a relaxed way but articulate it silently in your mind, 'Ma-ra-na-tha'.

Let the gift be given by God

To meditate well you need the quietest place you can find. You need a good posture, with your spine upright and calm and regular breathing.

Breathing – the simple rule is breathe. Do not get too het up about whether you should breathe in or breathe out. Do both!

Say your word, be content to say your word and let the gift be given by God. Meditation is very, very simple. Don't complicate it.

By your fidelity in returning to the mantra day after day, you root it in your heart and once rooted, it flourishes. Indeed it flowers.

Twenty minutes is the minimum time for meditation. Twenty-five or thirty minutes is about the average time.

From one-pointedness to infinite expansion

Why should breadth of vision arise from such narrowness of discipline?

The modern consciousness is not very keen on the idea of narrowness. Yet meditation is a way by which we focus our attention by *narrowing* our attention down to one point.

It might help to understand what meditation is about if it can be seen as a great double triangle:

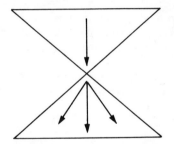

Here you have the triangle on the top, pointing down, and then the triangle underneath it, opening out. The triangle on the top is learning to concentrate, learning to focus our attention entirely upon and within Christ.

In that sense it is narrowing our attention to a single point. But as soon as we do so, the way is opened to infinite expansion on the other side.

A *change* of direction

There are no short-cuts. There are no crash courses. There is no instant mysticism. It is simply the gentle and gradual change of direction. The change of heart that comes is to stop thinking of yourself and to be open to God, to the wonder of him, to the glory of him and to the love of him.

There are many spiritual 'techniques' that promise 'instant' results. Any technique of prayer is by definition impatient – a disposable method, used until it produces a desired effect, then dropped and taken up again when we want more.

A technique is a goal-oriented thing, necessary if we are involved in learning how to drive a car or grow roses but disastrous if we are learning the way of unlearning, the way of prayer.

A technique in the realm of spirit intensifies our self-centredness. Meditation, in the Christian tradition, is so much more than a technique. It is to be understood as a discipline. It is a discipline in the richest and most positive sense of the word: a learning, a discipleship.

Does it make us think more about ourselves or less about ourselves? That is the Christian touchstone.

Our life must be in order

To pray, we need to be in the right frame of mind. Jesus used parables showing that moral smugness or resentment against another rendered prayer inauthentic, invalid.

Our 'right frame of mind', then, is not a mood or just getting the atmospherics nice. It is an openness of our whole person, demanding courage and perseverance.

It is no good having our 'spiritual' life in order – meditating twice a day or saying the Office together or any sort of practice of this kind – unless our practical life is equally in order and commensurate with it.

This great vision cannot be attained without commitment to small daily fidelities.

Let nothing be put before the work of God

Nearly everyone who came to the monastery asked what they should read on prayer and very few were content to be told to read nothing on prayer at all – until they had begun to meditate and discovered why. But we recommended a slow and careful reading of Scripture as an essential part of a mature Christian life.

I think it is a grave mistake to read too many books on prayer or on the spiritual life – time is so precious. It is much better to spend our time in meditation than reading someone who is writing about someone else's writing of what it is like to pray.

The call is not to be a great expert on all the latest paperbacks on spirituality. The call is to simple fidelity. 'Let nothing be put before the work of God' [The Rule of St Benedict]. Even the theory of the work of God.

The imagination is the great enemy of prayer. Reality is the presence of Jesus within us, the presence of his indwelling Spirit.

Wakefulness

Meditation has nothing to do with quiet reverie or passive stillness, but with wakefulness. We awaken to our nearness to God. We realize that the power of creation, the energy of creation, flows in our hearts.

Prayer, above all else, is not a nostalgia for God. Prayer is the summons to a full experience of the living Christ whose purpose, as St Paul tells us, 'is everywhere at work'.

That is why daydreaming is such a dreadful loss of opportunity, such a dreadful encapsulation in time.

St Paul's emphasis is not on religion as anaesthesia – thinking about the absent God and absenting ourselves from the present moment to be lost in a kind of pietistic dalliance. For Paul, the summons of the authentic religious intuition in humankind is to enter fully and courageously into the present moment, and there to be filled with life by the living Christ.

OUR LOVE FOR OTHERS IS THE
ONLY CHRISTIAN WAY OF
MEASURING OUR PROGRESS

Am I making progress?

When people ask how they can tell if they are making progress since they are not supposed to analyse or assess their actual periods of meditation, the answer is usually self-evident.

A greater rootedness in self, a deeper emotional stability, a greater capacity to centre in others and away from self are the signs of spiritual growth.

If you want to ask the question, 'Am I making progress?' do not look at your meditation. There is only one way we can judge our progress and that is by the quality of our love.

As the mantra leads us ever further from self-centredness we turn more generously to others and receive their support in return. Indeed, our love for others is the only truly Christian way of measuring our progress on the pilgrimage of prayer.

If we try to force the pace or to keep a constant self-conscious eye on our progress we are, if there is such a word, non-meditating because we are concentrating on ourselves, putting ourselves first, thinking about ourselves.

Freedom from ourselves

So often we think of ourselves as unworthy, but in the experience of prayer we must not think of ourselves at all. We must not think of our own unworthiness but we must *know* with utter clarity that the life of God is poured out into our hearts.

We must take up our cross and follow him. If we attempt to go for self-fulfilment, self-advancement, self-perfection, the only result can be *ruin*.

In meditation we turn the searchlight of consciousness off ourselves, off a self-centred analysis of our own unworthiness.

From illusion to reality

It is easy to read about wakefulness, to have elaborate and, as far as they go, accurate ideas about enlightenment, and yet all the while to be fast asleep.

The call to modern man, the call to all of us, is to become spiritual. To become spiritual we have to learn to leave behind our official religious selves – that is, to leave behind the Pharisee that lurks inside all of us – because, as Jesus has told us, we have to leave behind our whole self. All images of ourselves, coming as they do out of the fevered brain of the ego, have to be renounced and transcended if we are to become one with ourselves, with God, with our brethren – that is, to become truly human, truly real, truly humble.

Our images of God must similarly fall away. We must not be idol-worshippers. Curiously, what we find is that they fall away as our images of self fall away, which suggests what I suppose we always guessed anyway, that our images of God were really images of ourselves.

In this wonderful process of coming into the full light of Reality, of falling away from illusion, a great silence emerges from the centre. We feel ourselves engulfed in the eternal silence of God. We are no longer talking to God or worse, talking to ourselves. We are learning to be – to be with **God, to be in God**.

Contemplative vision necessary for contemporary action

Meditation is neither a backward glance nor a timorous projection forward but rather combines the old and the new in the glory of the eternal present – the 'perpetual now'. It is this element in meditation that makes the meditator a truly contemporary person, fully open and alive to the ever-present creative power of God sustaining the universe in being from moment to moment.

The liberty to 'move with the times', to recognize the changing needs and circumstances of the community or society around us, is the fruit of stability at the centre of our being.

It often seems to many people that prayer is an introspective state and that the meditator is someone going into himself to the exclusion of the people and creation around him, that he is socially irrelevant. Nothing could be further from the truth.

Not only is the timeless contemplative vision the necessary basis for contemporary action but it is the essential condition for a fully human response to life – to the richness, the unpredictability, the sheerly *given* quality of life.

To be with God

In meditation we go beyond thoughts, even holy thoughts. Meditation is concerned not with thinking but with being.

In contemplative prayer we seek to become the person we are called to be, not by thinking about God but by being with him. Simply to be with him is to be drawn into being the person he calls us to be.

This is no easy task for those of us reared in contemporary Western culture. We have all been conditioned by this culture's excessive regard for cerebral activity. And we have defined ourselves far too narrowly as 'rational creatures'. This is one of the principal reasons for the impoverishment of our prayer life. The response of the *whole person* to God has been shattered and only the cerebral, verbal splinters are active in our very attenuated understanding of prayer.

Our aim in Christian prayer is to allow God's mysterious and silent presence within us to become *the* reality which gives meaning, shape and purpose to everything we do, to everything we are.

The joy of being

Life in the dimension of Spirit is a mystery rooted in the joy of being.

The wonderful beauty of prayer is that the opening of our heart is as natural as the opening of a flower. To let a flower open and bloom it is only necessary to let it be, so if we simply *are*, if we become and remain still and silent, our heart cannot but be open, the Spirit cannot but pour through into our whole being. It is this we have been created for.

Our meditation teaches us that we have to put our whole heart into this work of the Spirit if we are genuinely to respond to the call to leave the shallows and enter into the deep, direct knowledge that marks a life lived in the mystery of God.

The call of Jesus is to worship God who is Spirit 'in Spirit and in Truth'.

These words of Jesus which we have perhaps listened to as an injunction should now be heard as a declaration of liberty.

An invitation to liberty

Meditation, as the way of life centred faithfully and with discipline on prayer, is our way into the true experience of spirit, of *the* Spirit. Anyone who follows this way soon comes to know for himself that its demand upon us increases with each step we take along the pilgrimage.

As our capacity to receive the revelation increases so too does the natural impulse we feel to make our response, our openness, more generous, more unpossessive.

The strange and wonderful thing is that this demand is unlike any other demand made upon us. Most demands upon us seem to limit our freedom, but this demand is nothing less than an invitation to enter into full liberty of spirit – the liberty we enjoy when we are turned away from self.

To understand this we cannot flinch from the fact that the demand is absolute, and consequently so must be our response.

Transformed from within

Meditation is a purifying process. In Blake's phrase, 'If the doors of perception were cleansed, everything will appear to man as it is, infinite' [*A Memorable Fancy: The Ancient Tradition*].

By means of the mantra we leave behind all passing images and learn to rest in the infinity of God himself. St Paul urges us to do just this when he implores us in Romans 12:

> . . . by God's mercy to offer your very selves to him, a living sacrifice, dedicated and fit for his acceptance, the worship offered by mind and heart. Adapt yourselves no longer to the pattern of this present world, but let your minds be remade and your whole nature thus transformed [Rm 12:1–2].

This transformation of our nature is put before us as a real and an immediate possibility. It is the essential Christian experience, the experience of being born again in the Holy Spirit, born again when we realize the power of the living Spirit of God within us.

The purification of our being

Learning to pray is learning to live as fully as possible in the present moment.

We may indeed begin meditating with a superficial concern for results, trying to estimate if our investment of time and energy is justified by returns in knowledge or 'extraordinary' experience. Perhaps anyone formed by our society is conditioned to begin in this way. But the ordinary practice of meditation purifies us of this spiritual materialism.

The hinge upon which we swing into the really transcendent experience is the fidelity and regularity of commitment that does not concern itself with 'good' meditations or 'bad' meditations.

The essential simplicity of simply saying the mantra; in this is the purification of our whole being.

Your faith will be strengthened

The time of meditation might often seem to you to be a complete waste of time, but only remember, Jesus dwells in your heart. Your faith will be tested and so your faith will be strengthened.

And so, make it the Way, the way you follow, leaving self behind and entering fully into the power of Christ's love. Everything else in your life flows from that personal encounter in your meditation because it is there that you find your own conviction.

Each time we meditate we return to the grounding consciousness of Being, and each time we return to the changing pattern of our life more firmly rooted in our being and so more able to perceive life as mystery and to communicate this perception in joy to others.

We have meaning for God

The wonder of love is that it always creates its own universe – we are explorers of a country without frontiers, one we discover little by little to be not a place but a person.

To meditate is to accept this exploration of the universe of God as the supreme meaning and authentication of our lives.

It is not simply that God is drawing us closer to himself by the revelation of his plan; it is rather that in Christ we are participating in the eternal meaning of the communion of love that is God.

Man is not meant to be a mere onlooker at this mystery. When the Creator, on the ceiling of the Sistine Chapel, passes his life into Adam, he looks into his inmost depths and from there he receives man's awakened recognition. God knows himself in man. We discover that we have meaning for God.

Becoming more loving

As St John tells us, no man has ever seen God, but we can all experience God whenever and wherever we encounter love. Jesus continues to communicate his presence to us in every way that people relate to one another in love.

Because meditation leads us into the experience of love at the centre of our being, it makes us more loving people in our ordinary lives and relationships.

You discover in the silence that you are loved and that you are lovable. It is the discovery that everyone must make in their lives if they are going to become fully themselves, fully human. The first step in personhood is to allow ourselves to be loved. To know ourselves loved is to have the depths of our own capacity to love opened up.

This condition of whole-hearted openness to love is the condition to which you and I and every human being is called. It demands everything. But in the end all you will lose are your limitations. So may we 'attain to fullness of being, the fullness of God himself' [Ep 3:19].

A MONASTERY IS A 'CENTRE OF PRAYER' ONLY TO THE DEGREE THAT IT IS A COMMUNITY OF LOVE

The monastic adventure

In a world increasingly ravaged by loneliness and isolation, the monastery is a practical demonstration that this is not the inevitable lot of man. It shows that we are called into the joy of being and in the living witness of flesh and blood it reveals being itself as communion.

A monastery is a place that testifies to the liberty of God to act as he will, to transcend the laws and conventions by which men limit the ordinary working of their lives and relationships.

A monastery is a 'centre of prayer' only to the degree that it is a community of love.

A monastery can serve the world only in proportion to its spirit of liberty and joy, the spirit of delirium arising from its knowledge that the Lord Jesus lives, and lives in our hearts.

The way of transcendence

St Benedict realized that he had located the essence of the spiritual life in his quest for purity of heart, the capacity to turn wholly and utterly away from self to the other, to a life of intimate union with God.

The renunciation of self-will that St Benedict envisages is not associated with a renunciation of the affections.

> The elder monks are to love the younger and the younger to obey the elder with all charity and all are to cherish fraternal love chastely as brothers [The Rule of St Benedict].

We can sense in this wonderfully human vision of a truly loving community something of the warmth of the southern Italian sun. So it is all the more remarkable that an Englishman like St Aelred of Rievaulx should have been able to incarnate this loving brotherhood in the most austere climes of Yorkshire. The thesis of his *De Amicitia Spirituale* is precisely that of exploring your relationship with God through human friendship.

The way of perfection in St Benedict's vision, therefore, is never the way of rejection but always the way of transcendence.

The necessary poverty of spirit

The monastic tradition has always emphasized, since Cassian and St Benedict, that poverty is the condition for prayer. The sanity of the tradition, its discipline and balance, has always been that it knew this poverty in prayer as the essential ascesis of the Christian life.

To worship means to bow and to bend low in spirit before the eternal, the spiritual, the reality that is God. The simple exercise of our repeated word brings us to that simplicity, the necessary poverty of spirit.

Silence releases the power of the glory of God in our heart. Indeed, we find the silence itself as power within us, the power of the Spirit who in silence is loving to all.

By stillness in the spirit we move in the ocean of God.

Preparation for prayer

Lectio (spiritual reading) prepares us for the mystery of God. We have to be clear that it prepares us. The movement itself is accomplished by the redemptive love of Jesus.

The monk is not trying to possess what he studies but uses his study to help him respond to the presence of God in his word. A loving reading and reflection upon the word of Scripture is, in Benedict's vision, essential in forming the monk as a man of prayer.

St Benedict saw *lectio* as an integral part of our Christian living. Why? Not because it made us better conversationalists or helped us pass exams. The purpose of *lectio* in the monastery is not the acquisition of knowledge. It is important to emphasize this because we have been trained to regard all education as the amassing of knowledge as a form of power.

Lectio is the great preparation for prayer that each monk builds into his life. It is also built into the corporate community life in the form of community *lectio* – what we know as the Divine Office.

The oblate community

In the old days there was a steady stream of young men who came to monasteries who could easily, in the very stable society that they came from, commit themselves to the monastery and to its work for life. It is unlikely, I think, that they will come in the future in great numbers.

Now in the way of the divine plan one door never closes without another door opening. I think that the oblate group attached to any monastery is going to assume an ever-greater importance in the future.

An oblate is a person who shares the ideals of the community and seeks to follow these ideals in the circumstances of his or her own life. The oblate group will not just be a pious group who associate themselves externally to the monastery and, as it were, bask in its reflected glory. The oblate group will be a group of mature, committed Christians who can share whole-heartedly in the teaching function of the monastery and in its single-minded pursuit of God.

The daily life of an oblate

We urge you to begin your day with morning prayer and your morning meditation and to end the day with evening prayer and your evening meditation. During the day read an excerpt from the Rule of St Benedict. Also, read something from the Bible, particularly from the New Testament. The community and the Scriptures are the great sources of strength for our pilgrimage.

As you read the Rule and see the great vision that St Benedict propounds, you will encounter your own weakness, your forgetfulness, your stupidity. The most difficult thing to put up with is your own stupidity. Do not be disheartened. St Benedict constantly urges us to start again.

One of the very practical things that he speaks of is not to allow the sun to go down on your anger. If you are angry, if you have a grudge against someone, if there is any lack of forgiveness in your heart, try to exorcize that before the sun goes down.

It is the gentleness of the Rule that is perhaps its most important characteristic for you as oblates.

Serious. Not solemn

It is not the great religious gestures that matter. So many of us are prepared to die for God as martyrs. We imagine colossal, dramatic scenes where we make our final speech from the dock or to the firing squad. I suppose, depending on our temperament, we are prepared for that.

But what St Benedict asks of us is something much more demanding – just to live our everyday life with simple fidelity.

When it comes to the time of our meditation or the Divine Office, we drop what we are doing and we go to it – simply. Not because abandoning what we are doing is a great act of service, but because the worship of God and living our lives on the bedrock of reality which is God, is of the most supreme importance. Not to do it would be stupidity. We need to be serious. Not solemn.

Advent – to prepare our hearts

If we are to know the truly spiritual quality of Christmas, the meaning of our celebration and ritual at home or in worshipping communities, we have to know what it means to enter into the space where celebration becomes possible with prepared, peaceful hearts.

This is one thing our daily pilgrimage of meditation teaches us from within. On that simple and humble journey we know what it means to make space in our heart, to prepare the heart for its great celebration of life.

It is only necessary for us to prepare our hearts to be prepared for everything. To leave behind the superficial is what we often mean by leaving behind the familiar. This can create a sense of emptiness as we become exposed to greater depth and more substantial reality.

Our coming home can seem like homelessness. Reflect a little this Christmas on the homelessness of the stable at Bethlehem.

Christmas – a season of our life

Christmas is a time when we become more sharply aware of the mysterious blend of the ordinary and the sublime in all life that is really Christian. It is important to see it as a blend, not as an opposition.

Christmas is the feast of great joy because our Redeemer comes. In all the great religious traditions, the Redeemer comes as a Child. He comes to restore to us our lost innocence, to restore us to a state of perfect childhood so that we are children of God, obedient to him, loving to him, anxious to serve him always as perfectly and as generously as we can.

A child's wonder and happiness at Christmas is very rightly seen as a sacrament of its real meaning. It is with the same simplicity that we should receive the supreme gift we receive in the love of Jesus.

Christmas is more than a feast. It is a season. And like all seasons, its essence is a cycle of preparation, achievement and then the incorporation of what has been achieved into the larger season of which it is a part, the season of our life.

The spirit of Lent

As we prepare to enter another Lent let us keep one another in our hearts. This is a time of conversion – a time to turn from what is passing away in order to be at one with him who is eternal.

Base your life on that spirit of conversion. Everything else flows from that – what we should do, where we should go. It requires courage. It requires a truly virile spirit not to sink back into the easy options of egoism, not to be content just to get through our lives but to live them to the full with joy, with enthusiasm and with a real sense of the fun of life flowing from that liberty.

Lent is not a time for self-important beating of our breast and lamenting over our sinfulness. Lent is a time to prepare for the glory of Christ, the glory of Easter, the paschal glory. We do so, not by concentrating on our own sinfulness, but by forgetting ourselves and by opening our hearts to the Lord Christ.

Easter – a living mystery

The mystery is Jesus: risen, glorious, fully alive.

It is a living mystery that overflows the normal demarcations of our thought and feeling and transcends the capacity of human structure or organization to contain or direct it.

Real and powerful as is the presence of Jesus in our hearts and wonderful as is the transformation it can effect, it does not impose itself on us by force – because it is love. It will not break through the door of our heart. We must open our heart to it.

The Kingdom of God is simply God's power enthroned in our hearts. Faith in the 'Kingdom of God' is what makes us light of heart and is what Christian joy is about.

Infinite expansion of spirit

The Kingdom of Heaven is among us and we must be open to it now. As St Peter says, we must be alive in the Spirit and become fully alive with the life of God. As Christians we must never settle for less.

Christian life is not a question of just getting through our lives; every word of the New Testament suggests to us that it is of supreme importance that we live our lives in a state of continuous expansion of heart and spirit, growing in love and becoming more firmly rooted in God.

Above all, know from your own heart, from your own experience, that you were created for infinite expansion of spirit. Every act of faith is a step into the infinite expansion of God.

Sources and Index

LH: *Letters from the Heart* (New York, Crossroad 1982. By permission of the publishers)
MC: *Moment of Christ* (NY, Crossroad 1984)
PC: *The Present Christ* (NY, Crossroad, 1984)
WS: *Word into Silence* (NY, Paulist Press 1981)

Published by The Benedictine Priory of Montreal:

CL: *Community of Love* (1984)
CMed: *Christian Meditation* (1977)
CMys: *Christian Mysteries* (1979)
DIJ: *Death: The Inner Journey* (1983)
HP: *The Hunger for Prayer* (1983)
MA: *The Monastic Adventure* (1983)
MPMM: *Monastic Prayer and Modern Man* (1983)
OCM: *The Other-Centredness of Mary* (1983)
PL: Personal letter, 12 Oct. 1976, published by permission of Father Laurence Freeman.

In the index which follows, the figures in bold type refer to pages of the present book.